PENNIES
from
RAVEN

NANCY KENNEDY

WESTBOW
PRESS®
A DIVISION OF THOMAS NELSON
& ZONDERVAN

WestBow Press books may be ordered through booksellers or by contacting:

WestBow Press
A Division of Thomas Nelson & Zondervan
1663 Liberty Drive
Bloomington, IN 47403
www.westbowpress.com
844-714-3454

ISBN: 978-1-6642-3371-3 (sc)
ISBN: 978-1-6642-3370-6 (e)

Print information available on the last page.

WestBow Press rev. date: 07/07/2021

CONTENTS

INTRODUCTION

Pennies, who'd of ever thought they could mean so much. Over the years, I've found them here and there, with no real concern of what they might mean, or what they might be saying. It wasn't until Padrick and I lost our only child that we learned through a friend how wonderful "penny finds" can really be. Now we catch ourselves seeking them out, but it's only when we're not looking that they fall onto our paths, at the most unexpected times, in the most unexpected of places. As I write, it's been just over 10 years since we lost Raven, and I honestly haven't counted exactly how many pennies we've found since she left us for Heaven, but I journal about each one, where it was found and who found it. Sometimes others share with us their penny finds, and how they're reminded of Raven when they do. Seems she leaves penny signs of her presence for so many, even some we don't know personally, but they've learned of our story. Raven just likes letting us all know that she's alright and that she'll see us again one day on the other side of the clouds. I do miss her so much, Padrick and I both do. I remember a dream he had of her that he shared with me not long after her accident. In his dream he was deep in grief and crying over the loss of Raven. He called out to her loudly,

"Come home Raven!" He said he kept saying it over and over, begging her to come back home. It was then she said back to him in the dream, "I am home daddy." Tears filled his eyes as he shared the dream with me. Tears welled up in my eyes too, and they still do every time I sit and really think about that dream, he shared with me. As hard as life has been for us living in Raven's absence, we do have a peace in knowing that she is home, she's in her eternal home, one we aspire to be, one where we anticipate a sweet reunion with her when God decides to call us home too. We cling to the hope we have of seeing Raven again. It's what sees us in and out of each passing day. Although it feels like forever this side of Heaven, we trust a day is coming when we will weep no more, our joy will finally come. For now, we'll hold every penny she tosses down as a precious treasure and a reminder that we're only just a heartbeat away.

1

A Storm Was Brewing

I've always heard it said that in life we all have storms. We're either headed for one, in the midst of one, or coming out of one. Sometimes they come with warnings to kindly prepare us, other times they'll just hit unexpectedly out of nowhere, wounding us in ways we never imagined. These are the ones we fear most. These are the ones we consider and categorize to be our worst nightmares. These are the ones we try hardest not to think about, knowing full well the possibilities of the realities each could become.

It's funny how sometimes we try convincing ourselves that bad things only happen to "other people." Whatever makes us think so highly of ourselves to even consider such a thing? What a fairytale that is. In the Bible, the book of Matthew Chapter 5 verse 45 tells us that God sends rain on the just and the unjust. Even if we manage to keep our heads dry, everybody's feet will get wet eventually. I can't help but think of Job and all that he endured. God allowed him to be tested way beyond what many of us will ever experience. He lost his wealth and all 10 of his children in one day, and as if that were not enough for, he and his wife to suffer through, God allowed a second storm to come and attack Job's body. Verse 7 in Chapter 2 of the book of Job says that he was afflicted with painful sores from the top of his head to the soles of his feet. Already suffering mentally in deep grief over the loss of his children and worldly possessions, he was now physically impaired, his body and spirit broken. Even Jobs wife, his helpmate, was unable to offer up comfort or encouragement as she too suffered greatly in their loss. I can only imagine the degree of devastation they felt and the questions that must have filled their minds.

It seems that almost daily we hear news of loss and suffering in the world. If not ourselves, I'm sure that each of us know of someone engaged in a battle, whether it be mental, physical or spiritual. I've always been a pretty cautious person, even more so as I've aged, always running the "what ifs" through my mind as if somehow that gives me a head start on preparing for the unexpected. I can remember one day at work as I was traveling down Brice's Store Road just backside of the feed mill from where I work, and randomly thinking to myself, "What would I do if anything ever happened to my husband Padrick or my daughter Raven?" I was immediately overcome with tears, followed by a quick sweep of nausea and the feeling of being punched in the stomach. For some reason Raven just really burned in my mind, and even the thought of possibly losing her was heartbreaking. Now, I realize you're wondering, "What about her husband?" To answer that question, "Yes, I would be crushed at the loss of him too." After all, he is half of Raven, but for some reason that day it became more about

Raven. Did God plant that seed in my mind to prepare me for something ahead? I didn't know, I hoped not.

Being a mother, I can attest to the fact that mothers do worry over their children. We pray earnestly for them, but then there's a natural tendency to worry too. I prayed over Raven daily, while at the same time keeping my phone always in arms reach during those times, we were apart. I can remember once when she was about 15 years old. Padrick had gone to the mountains with his family, and because I had to work that weekend, Raven stayed home with me. That evening, she'd asked if she could go with some friends to Mikes Tree Farm for a haunted hayride. It was October, and the weather was nice out. I wasn't really thrilled about letting her venture off to anything haunted, but I eventually caved into her request. I drove her to the next town over where her friends picked her up, and we agreed to meet at the same place a few hours later so that I could pick her up and bring her back home. I later found myself sitting in the living room at our house, watching tv and holding my phone incase Raven called. I was still in my work uniform, carrying the faint smell of hog on my clothes, yet daring not to get a shower for fear of missing any calls from Raven. With Padrick gone out of town for the weekend, I felt that I needed to be ready in the event any emergency situation should arise concerning Raven. After what felt like forever and a day, Raven finally called for me to pick her up, only she wasn't where we'd agreed to meet at earlier, nor did she go to the place she'd originally intended. I was not happy about the change of plans, nor her failure to inform me sooner. I gave her no option but to be back at the place we'd agreed to meet, and once I got her in my truck, the lecture began. Through angry tears, I did my best to explain to her why any change of plans were important to share with me, and I reminded her of exactly why Padrick and I paid for her to have a cell phone, eliminating her excuse of, "I had to go where the people I was riding with went." I rehearsed with her how I would have driven in the wrong direction had she been involved in an accident, assuming she were in one place, and not knowing all the while she was miles away in another. I guess teenagers don't think about things like that. I probably didn't either at that age.

I believe in times of trouble that God prompts us to pray for the needs of others, even if we don't know exactly what those needs are. Years ago, when Raven was still in elementary school, I can remember of a particular time when God prompted me to pray for her. I was clueless of exactly what was going on with Raven at that very moment, but I was obedient to God's call for me to pray earnestly over her. I felt an urgency in my spirit to pray like never before, and God gave me a sudden peace in knowing He was protecting her from whatever had the potential to cause her harm. Here I was, driving along doing my job, getting the hogs fed, and God randomly jolts me to give Him all I've got in prayer over my daughter. Of course, I did exactly what He'd asked, and I did it without delay. Praying over Raven was something I did daily anyway, but this time it was different. It's like God was warning me that she was in danger, I honestly believe that with all my heart. That evening when I picked her up from school, I asked her about her day, and all that she'd done. She shared with me that at recess she'd climbed up on top of the monkey bars and walked across the top of them. Almost immediately, in my mind I began to picture how deadly a potential fall could have been for Raven, and I realized that the time God prompted me to pray for her was about the same time she'd been outside for recess. I was thankful for God's protection over her, yet angry that any supervising adult could have overlooked the dangerous situation Raven had put herself in. Looking back, I try to put myself in that person's shoes, with so many students and so many distractions, I see now why God got my attention to pray that day.

It's amazing how life can suddenly change. Things as we know them to be. The comfort of routine, the pre-planned activities we anticipate coming without interruption. We live by the clock and the calendar, and we try so hard to fit each day's activity into our own little mold. We plan for our futures with no regard for the present. We look so far ahead that we don't really enjoy the moment we're in. I can't help but think of what the Bible tells us in James Chapter 4:13-15. It's a reminder that we none know what tomorrow holds, and that it is God's will that prevails, not ours. God doesn't promise any of us a set number of tomorrows. It is He and He alone who determines our days. In the book of Jeremiah Chapter 1 verse 5, we learn that before God even formed us in our mother's womb, he knew us. Luke 12:7 tells us that God knows the very hairs on our heads. Job 14:5 reminds us that our days in this life are determined by God and that it is He who decrees our time and sets our limits. Nothing happens in our lives without God's knowledge or permission, and no matter how good you think you've been or how closely connected you feel in your faith, the storms of life will come. Are you prepared?

When I sit and think about what God looks like, I see

in my mind a picture of "The Little Mermaid's" father from the Disney movie that came out so many years ago. I picture God to look physically strong, having abs of steal and the arms of a body builder. I picture him with long, gray hair depicting his wisdom and glory. I imagine the sound of his voice to be deep and the pronunciation of His words to be clearly heard with no need of repeating. I consider myself to have a healthy fear and respect for God, and I am fully aware that He is in control of everything. I believe He has reasons for what He allows in our lives even when we can't see them or understand why. I trust Him completely. Being I can hide nothing from God, I realize my life is an open book to Him. He knows every chapter, how it all started and exactly how and when it will end. When the storms in our lives come, He is there, even for those that come without warning. I look back now and picture Him looking down at me and Padrick, pointing His finger over our lives, and slowing making a circling motion. Unbeknownst to us, the clouds started closing in. A storm was brewing.

2

THE WORST DAY EVER

Sunday January 24, 2010 started out like any other day. I'd been working mandatory extra shifts for a while, but I was hopeful to soon see my Sundays off again in the near future. My alarm clock sounded at 3:50am, I got up, got ready for work, did my exercises, ate some breakfast, and walked into Raven's room while she slept, kissed her forehead and told her that I loved her. I did this every morning before I left for work. Padrick walked me to the door, kissed me goodbye, and we exchanged "I Love You's" as I turned to leave for the day. On the way to my truck I grabbed the "House for Sale" sign up out of our front yard, and I put it in our garage, somewhat relieved that we'd be staying in our house. Forty days prior, Padrick and I had decided to try to sell our house for financial and relocation reasons. We prayed about it and decided to give it 40 days. We believed that if it were God's will for us to move, within 40 days someone would show interest and buy our house, if not, it was His will that we stay put. Either way, we trusted that God knew best. In the 40 days, we had a few calls, and one no-show, but no real potential buyers. Ironically, just the night before, the story that went with our devotional for our Family Scripture Time together was about a couple trying to sale their house. As a family of 3, it was obvious neither of us were really sad about the fact that on one wanted to buy our house. We love it, so that's all that really mattered. We had no real problem staying where we were. The 40 days had passed, so we believed that it was God's will, and who could argue with that?

It was Men's Day at our church that day. I was sorry to be missing it because of work, but happy to see that I'd gotten a load to Maple Hill Sow. With it, I could swing through Chinquapin on my way to catch a few minutes with Padrick and Raven. I knew that church would be letting out around the same time I'd be coming through. Padrick and Raven had driven separately, and Raven was the first to get home. Padrick was soon to follow. The night before, Raven, with our permission had made plans to spend the afternoon riding 4-wheelers with her friends; something she'd done numerous times before. Glad I'd caught her before she left for the day, I gave her a kiss, told her to be careful and to be home before our Youth meeting that evening at church. She assured me she'd be back in time. She gave Padrick a kiss and was on her way. Soon after she left, Padrick walked me back out to my truck. About that time, we heard the alarm go off at the Fire Department. Being Raven was gone, of course we were concerned. We said a little prayer and a few minutes later, Padrick called me to let me know that Raven was safe and sound at Bojangles and having herself a little something to eat before venturing out to ride 4-wheelers for the day. Relieved that all was well with her, I was back to feeding the hogs, and looking forward to the end of a Sunday shift in what I like to call "The Chamber."

On my way home from work, I found myself mentally preparing for what I consider my Second Shift or Round 2 of the day. I had a window of time to eat supper, get to choir practice and later conduct a Youth meeting with our teens at church. Would I have time to shower, or would I have to like so many times before, go to church smelling like hogs? The thoughts that ran through my mind had me in a mental countdown, a race against the clock. I gave myself an E for effort. I figured God favored timeliness over cleanliness, unlike Padrick. He takes no liking to my work uniform, or the smell it brings home every day.

As I got closer to home, I drove past the Fire Department, and I couldn't help but to notice that an ambulance was pulling out. The lights were going, but no alarm was sounding. I said a little prayer for the responders and whomever they were responding to. I thought it was strange that there was no alarm, so I assumed that maybe the call they'd gotten wasn't necessarily a dire emergency. I pulled into our driveway a minute or so later, relieved to finally be home and hungry for whatever Padrick was cooking for supper. I unlaced my work boots, came in the back door and laid my phone and wallet down on the kitchen counter. It seemed just seconds later my phone rang. As I turned to reach for it, Padrick said he'd get it, so I decided to go ahead and get my hands washed up for supper. Listening, in my mind I was trying to guess who was calling, and it was then I noticed a look of panic on Padrick's face as I heard him ask, "Is she ok?" He repeated the question over and over and I immediately said, "It's Raven, something happened to Raven!" It's like I knew. I was sure in that moment that something really bad had happened to Raven, and I was instantly consumed with fear. Panicked, I grabbed my keys and wallet, slid my boots back on, and ran back out to my truck. I got inside, cranked it up and started backing out of our driveway, clueless as to exactly where I should be heading. Padrick came running out to the driveway to stop me. He jumped in on the passenger's side and said, "Raven's been in an accident, go to Riley's house!" Hearing him say those words just confirmed what I already thought. My state of panic immediately kicked into overdrive. All I could think about was getting to where Raven was as fast as I could. I felt like I was in a race to get to Riley's house, and I began praying that Raven was ok. It's all I could do at that moment, drive and pray.

Riley was one of Raven's friends, he was with her, and it was he who had made the call. In route to his house, we soon found ourselves behind the same ambulance I'd seen just minutes prior on my way home from work. At this point it was moving at a leisurely speed with no lights or siren sounding. It sparked even more anxiety in me, and I began making assumptions, asking myself and Padrick, "Is this ambulance responding to Raven?" If it is, maybe it's going slow because she's alright and they don't need it, or maybe it's because she's not alright. We followed behind it the whole way to Riley's house, even as it passed by, we followed it all the way out to the main highway. There was no one at Riley's house, so at that point neither Padrick nor myself knew where to go. I told him to call Riley back, totally confused as to why we'd been instructed to go somewhere Raven wasn't even at. It was some time later Padrick told me that the reason he said to go to Riley's house was off the assumption that it was where Raven was, being he was one of the friends she'd be riding 4-wheelers with that day. I guess we both just figured she'd be somewhere in the woods down by his house, and in our panic we neither one thought to ask exactly where they were. What we gathered from that was that they were somewhere off a path on Hallsville Road. As we drove, we started looking down every dirt path we saw, but nothing! I was sick to my stomach over the time we were wasting looking in all the wrong places. I don't know why, but I pulled over on the shoulder of the road, got out of my truck and started running down the highway. Not knowing where to find Raven was literally taking my breath. My heart was pounding, and I was exasperated to the point I thought I was going to have a heart attack. Padrick slid over to the driver's side of my truck, drove to me and said, "Nancy, you've got to calm down, we'll find her!" I got back inside, and just a little further down the road, we saw someone standing on the shoulder as if they wanted us to stop. A man there informed us of a bad accident down the road. Padrick told him that our daughter was in an accident, and that we were trying to find her. Relived to finally get some direction as to where she might be, we drove on ahead to find a crowd of people and vehicles parked all around the entrance of a wooded path off the highway.

I saw Raven's friend Riley there at the road on his 4-wheeler. Before Padrick could even fully stop the truck, I jumped out and ran over to where Riley was. I asked, "Riley, where's Raven?" He told me that she was still back in the woods and that there were people with her. With that said, I was able to calm down to some degree. I asked Riley if he would take me to Raven on his 4-wheeler, and he said that he would. With my face full of tears and buried in his back, I wondered why he was driving so slowly. As I continued praying in my mind and asking God that she be alright, I wondered why and how Riley could be so quiet. He said nothing to calm me and gave me no insight to the extent of Raven's injuries.

When we finally stopped, I lifted my head and started looking for Raven. I noticed an orange sheet on the ground over to my left by a ditch, and there was an ambulance to my right. I ran over to the ambulance and asked the responders, "Where's Raven, I'm her mother, where is she?" One of the EMT personnel pointed over to the orange sheet I'd seen laying on the ground and said, "She's over there." I ran over to the orange sheet. I could see Raven's hair under it and her boots sticking out from underneath on the other end. Her body had been covered up by the sheet and her face too. Confused as to why no one was attending to her and why her face was covered up by the sheet, I reached down, grabbed hold of it and snatched it back. What I saw in that moment broke my heart into a thousand pieces. There was my Raven, her face swollen almost beyond recognition with blood covering her nose and mouth. Her body looked as if it had been slammed into a brick wall. I could literally feel the life leaving my body. No one was trying to help her, and I didn't want to know the real reason as to why. I didn't want to believe that what I was seeing was real. I put my hands-on Raven's face, and it was still warm. I bent down to her nose, no breath. I starred at her chest waiting to see if it would rise and fall, but nothing. No sign of life. I knew in my mind she was gone, but my heart was in denial, and it felt as if slowly it were being ripped from my chest. It wasn't long when I turned to see Padrick standing there behind me. I'll never forget the look on his face. He was frozen. He just stood there, silent and broken. Our worst nightmare had suddenly become our reality. Our only child, our world, our everything gone! I remember words being spoken by those around us, but in that moment it's like none of them could really be heard. It was like watching a tragic scene in a movie with the volume turned down low.

Sometime later Padrick and I were asked to step away from the accident scene. Raven was loaded up into an ambulance, and we were told that we could follow along behind as they took her to a nearby hospital. I asked the leading EMT attendant permission for Padrick and I to ride on the ambulance with Raven. He explained that no passengers were allowed to ride, but after much begging on my part, he made an exception of mercy with the promise that I would make every effort I could to maintain my composure. As Padrick and I entered into the ambulance, seeing Raven's lifeless body in the light brought even more confirmation to what we already knew. I remember sitting with my knees at her head and holding it in the palms of my hands as we traveled the long, bumpy, dirt road back towards the highway. Padrick sat to Ravens left, and I could hear him whispering what sounded like a prayer. I began to notice that with every bump we hit along the path, a fresh flow of blood from Ravens nose would surface. A spark of hope for life in her arose in my mind, and I asked the woman riding in the back of the ambulance with us if the blood flow could possibly mean that Raven was still alive. She told me that it was only a result of the bumps in the road, and she began wiping around Ravens nose and mouth with a towel. I continued to stare at Ravens chest for any sign of movement, desperately hoping to prove the EMT Attendant wrong, but once again, nothing. After what felt like a 30-minute ride, we finally made it back out to the main road. The ambulance stopped for a few seconds, and we saw the faces of some waiting look in through the rear windows at us. A friend made eye contact with me, and I remember with a deep expression of sadness, she mouthed the words, "I love you."

The ride to the hospital was quite; no one said a word. Once we arrived, Padrick and I were escorted to a waiting area, then to the chapel where we were met by family and friends there to offer their love and sympathies. I remember going to the restroom and looking up in the mirror at myself, feeling my greatest heartbreak and now seeing it reflected back to me. I was in shock, broken and numb. I remember my friend Freda praying over us that night. It was a powerful, heartfelt prayer that I knew was being delivered for a specific restoration purpose. It was spoken with such urgency and command, as if our very survival was dependent on it, and somehow in my spirit, I knew it was. I felt the presence of God in her prayer. I understood without question that this tragedy in losing Raven so unexpectedly was a direct attack from Satan on my faith, my marriage, and my family. I believe Freda knew that, and I now know that it was spoken on behalf of Padrick and myself with the soul intent to prepare us for a spiritual battle neither of us could have ever imagined.

As family and friends continued to pour in at the hospital, the reality of the events of the evening became more real. I literally felt like I had just kissed Raven goodbye that morning, and here we were just a few hours later in a place none of us expected to be. A nurse approached Padrick and I in the hallway of the hospital and asked if we'd like to see Raven, and of course we said yes. Unaware that we'd seen her at the accident site already, as well as rode with her on the ambulance to the hospital, she gently and sympathetically assumed her duty to warn us of what Raven's appearance would be like. We then shared the fact that we'd just been with her, and we were prepared for what we'd see. My parents walked back with us, and the nurse led us outside to a small room at the back of the building where Ravens body lay. She was partially covered in a black bag with her face and hair exposed. I remember watching my daddy as he approached her lifeless body and how he just broke down in tears, we all did. Unbelievable! That's what is was, unbelievable! Our only child, their only grandchild, gone.

The nurse who attended to us gave me an envelope with Ravens things in it, her earrings, chap stick, class ring and gum. Her cell phone was still working, even after being in a ditch of water tucked into the pocket of her pants. I feel like it was protected for our benefit. It held her voicemail, her last pictures, and a few of her favorite songs. A friend of Ravens who'd been with her that day kept telling Padrick and I that Raven was having a good time. I guess he felt that somehow it would soften the blow for us, but it didn't, not for me anyway. In that moment my concern wasn't in the fact that Raven was having fun with her friends before she died, but that she died. She died! There was no warning, no time to prepare, no nothing! She was snatched from our lives without even a goodbye. She took her last breath in this world a mile or so back in the woods on the shoulder of a dirt path, and neither Padrick or myself were there to hold her, to hug and kiss her one last time before she transitioned from this world to the next. I have pictured that scene in my mind thousands of times, and it still bothers me. Although I'm grateful she had her friends by her side and others to assist her in her final moments of life, it's agonizing to live with no goodbye. I can look back now and appreciate knowing she was having fun with her friends, but the tragic ending leaves me feeling so undone even to this day.

As we prepared to leave the hospital that night, Padrick and I realized we'd left my truck by the road across from the path where Raven had her accident, so a family friend drove us home. On the way, I called my supervisor to let him know what had happened, but he already knew. I had no clue of when I'd be mentally or physically able to return to work, Padrick didn't either. It was a long, quite ride home, just like the ride from Ravens accident site to the hospital on the ambulance. I remember my mama coming over to spend the night. We both laid in Ravens bed, a place she'd just been sleeping the night before. Padrick was across the hall in our bed. We all pretty much cried ourselves to sleep, wishing it was a bad dream and we'd wake up the next day with Raven still with us, alive and thriving, getting herself ready for another day at school, but the bad dream was real. We knew we'd be waking up only to relive our worst nightmare, our new reality. Raven was gone, never to return to us again. Our hearts were broken.

3

THE DAY AFTER

The next morning was a blur. We'd none had any rest or gotten any real sleep. Less than 24 hours prior, Raven and Padrick were up getting themselves ready for church. I was at work, and all was well with our world. Now here we were, trying to pull ourselves together to meet at the funeral home to plan and prepare for Ravens memorial service. How did we go from "all is well" to this unexpected loss? How did we get here?

As we stumbled around, smothered in grief, we tried with all we had to gather ourselves together to meet the needs the day demanded. The phone calls and house visits started up, and food started coming in by the arms full. For some reason the flow of people and food was directed to my parent's house, we never really figured out why, we just somehow managed being between our house and theirs.

When the time came for us to leave for the funeral home, we all gathered up into the Expedition. I remember Padrick's nephew driving us there, and just like the day before, the ride was long and quiet. Other family members followed close behind us, none of us ever imagined ourselves preparing to plan a funeral service that day. We were all floored by the unexpected blow of Raven's sudden death. The life of a healthy, vibrant sixteen-year-old taken without warning. We realize the possibility that death can bring to each new day, but even knowing that in no way prepared any of us for such a loss. Driving up to the funeral home brought us to a playing field we weren't equipped for. Raven was our only child, she was our future, and now memories of her would be all we had left. I could hardly believe what we were about to have to do, and even to this day, I still try pretending it's all just a bad dream.

Once inside the funeral home, we were led to a room I'd never been in before, and I had attended countless services there over the years. Here we were, on the other side of the wall in the planning room. Although there was discussion prior to, I felt like most of the decisions to be made were up to me. Padrick was so broken, he told me to do whatever I wanted to. He did request no autopsy for Raven. We discussed cremation and having her ashes split up between an urn to be buried in the church cemetery and an ash box for her room. To our surprise the funeral director and his wife, people we knew well, personally covered the cost of the ash box we selected for Raven. Everything that had to be taken care of that day was handled with a great deal of care. It was surely something no parent should ever have to do. It's just not the normal order of things. Parents are not supposed to outlive their children. We tend to live our lives as if things like this only happen to other people, and here we found ourselves to be the other people.

While at the funeral home that day, Padrick and I were

asked if we'd like to see Raven one last time. I did, Padrick chose not to. He said he didn't want to remember her that way. As I walked into the room where her body lay, I was accompanied by some family and a friend. I could see that she still had leaves and straw from the accident site entangled in her hair. By this point her face was even more swollen, and her skin was purple. It was so hard seeing her look that way, but I couldn't imagine not taking one last opportunity to see her and kiss her. As I leaned down to kiss her face, I felt the coldness of her body on my lips, and my heart sank in my chest. I'd just kissed her face twice the day before, and she was warm with life. It felt like our lives had just been turned upside down, everything good was gone in an instant.

After making all of Raven's arrangements at the funeral home, there was still much to do at home, and all of that became a juggling act between the constant stream of visitors and phone calls. We truly appreciated that others wanted so badly to express their sympathies in our loss, but it was very challenging to get all that we had to get done with so many distractions. We felt an obligation to be as attentive as possible to each and every visitor. It was obvious that Raven's life and death touched many people. We were so grateful to see just how loved and missed she already was.

Those first 24 hours after required so much more of Padrick and I that we were mentally prepared for. We were both still so much in shock and broken beyond repair. Confirmation of Ravens death hit us at every angle with news reports on the television and in local newspapers, not to mention the countless Facebook post others kept us informed of. There were moments we found ourselves pausing to catch a breath from it all. At times I found myself wondering how many people found out before we did as the news of Ravens death spread fast.

So many stories circulated as to exactly what happened that day. I wanted explicit detail, Padrick didn't. We were told by the EMT responders that Raven died instantly, however we soon found out that was not exactly true. A day or so after her accident, a man who was there that day shared his witness of Ravens final moments of life. He came by my parent's house an evening or so after, and he told Padrick and I that he was with Raven that day and wanted to share with us what he'd seen and done for her to help that day. We all stepped out on my parent's front porch away from the crowd, and he began to tell us everything he remembered. We hung on every word he spoke. He said that he and his brother were there that day riding too, and that they'd driven up on the scene of Ravens accident just moments after. He shared that Raven and Michael, the young man Raven was with, were both thrown into a ditch. They could see that Raven was seriously injured, so they hurriedly, but carefully carried her up out of the ditch and moved her to the shoulder. He said that Raven was conscious and able to speak, but she appeared seriously hurt. He then told Ravens friend Riley to call Padrick and I. As he spoke, he said Raven looked up at him as if to be listening in on what he'd told her friend Riley. He shared with us that it was then Raven spoke the words, "Love you," and just seconds later she stopped breathing. Hearing this brought an ocean of tears to our eyes as Raven was known to say, "Love you," not "I Love You." It was as if she already knew she'd be gone by the time we got to where she was, and she wanted us to know that she loved us. The man and his brother began to perform CPR on Raven, but there was no response. I believe they did all that they could that day to help save Raven, but God already had other plans.

I've always believed that when it's our appointed time to die, that nothing and no one on earth can stop it. If our love and prayers could have saved Raven, she'd still be here. Chapter 139 verse 16 in the book of Psalms attest to that. God ordained for Raven to live in this world 16 years, 5 months and 14 days. When she woke up the morning of Sunday, January 24th she was clueless that it would be her last, we none knew. Every day I prayed for God to camp His angels of protection around her. When I envision that evening in my mind, I see those angels suddenly withdrawn as Raven enters the curve. In that moment, life as we'd known it was changed. Nothing would ever be the same again.

"Love you" memorialized on Raven's Jeep Liberty front plate.

4

Six Months In

The first few months following Ravens death were filled with continuous visits, phone calls and countless, comforting and sympathetic cards. Seems there was always something to attend, somewhere to be, or something to be done. I found myself loaded up on speaking engagements and singing opportunities, all of which I did my best to accept and deliver. People seemed so eager to hear about Raven's accident and how Padrick and myself were doing, how we were surviving in our loss. It was only the grace of God and the prayers of others that carried us in and out of each passing day, and we were fully aware of that.

We noticed at about 6 months in that things were beginning to slow down. The phone got quiet, the visits lessoned, and the flow of cards no longer filled our box at the post office. It was back to just bills and donation requests. The reality of what would now be our new normal began to sink in. Coming home to a quiet house after a long day at work seemed so odd. Raven was very active in sports, so we were always on the go to a practice or a game which kept us busy and mobile. Now here we were with nowhere to be. It was just me and Padrick trying desperately to figure out how to plug up this big hole that Raven's death had left in our lives. We continued to support the school sports teams that Raven had been a part of, and we were honored to see the effort made on their part to keep her memory alive. The boys' varsity soccer team had dedicated their entire season to Raven and even made it to the state playoffs. We truly appreciated everything that was done for Raven during basketball, soccer and tennis seasons, but it was still so hard for us knowing that she couldn't physically be a part of it all. We struggled way beyond what we allowed others to see, and still do.

Looking back now, I realize those first six months of preoccupation with people and things to distract us was God's way of keeping Padrick and I afloat. At times I actually felt an obligation to entertain when people came to visit and spend time with us. I wanted them to be comfortable and feel welcome, yet at the same time I found myself sporting a fake smile, pretending it was all a bad dream, that Raven was still here and would come back home soon. I refer to that as "running the plastics," trying so hard to hold myself together when inside I was falling apart.

As the newness of Ravens death began to wear off for others, Padrick and I found ourselves still in shock from it all. It was so hard coming to terms with the fact that Raven, our only child was suddenly gone. Life as we knew it to be was changed forever, and there was absolutely nothing we could do to get it back as it was. Waking up to her absence everyday became more and more of a confirmation that she wasn't coming back, and my ability to pretend that she was became more and more of a mental struggle. The physical effects of grief brought a morning punch in the stomach and countless sweeps of nausea with each passing day. The flow of tears forced me to keep a paper towel on hand at all times. Most anything could trigger a wave in me, a song, a favorite food of Ravens, the color orange, just random things that somehow connected my thoughts of Raven and all the things that she loved. Every moment of the day was filled with memories of her and all that once was. I found myself counting the days, weeks, and months that had passed since we'd last seen her, and as time moved on in life for everyone else, I wanted nothing more than to go back to the way things were. I held on to the past with everything that I had, because to me, no matter what came into our lives from then on, it would never compare to life with Raven.

In our seasons of tremendous heartache and sadness, I believe God purposely places us in just the right location at just the right time. He knows what we need and exactly when to deliver. He knows just how much we can and cannot bear. 1 Corinthians Chapter 10 verse 13 testifies to that. Forty days after Ravens accident I'd gone back to work on the truck, but against Padrick's wishes. Being alone most of my workday, he's concluded that it would not be beneficial to my mental state, however, surprisingly as hard as it was for me, the alone time became somewhat of an escape. I could cry, scream out to God, do anything I wanted to release the anger my grief brought, and no one was there to interrupt it or judge me. Something about being back at work strangely brought with it a little normalcy to life.

Every day while at work, around 2:45pm, Raven would

call me to talk about her plans after school, and not getting that call anymore at that time of day was heartbreaking. I found myself calling her phone so many times, wishing so much that she would answer, but realizing she never would again.

August 2010 brought new job opportunities to Padrick. Unhappy with where he was, he began to seek out other avenues of employment. Having his Business Degree completed, his resume now held that one thing so many potential employers were looking for. Padrick, had applications submitted for several different jobs he found interest in. One day he happened to run into a friend who shared of an opening at the school by our house, practically in our back yard, and one Raven had attended for 9 years of her life. God was opening up a door for Padrick, actually 2 doors were opened, but it was up to him to decide. One job was a good drive away but offered great pay, the other was walking distance from home, less pay, and required a little more education. After weighing out the pros and cons of each, lots of prayer and seeking God's direction, we both decided the school was where he needed to be. It wasn't long before he transitioned from his current job and became a Health and Physical Education teacher for Elementary and Jr. High students at Chinquapin School. Once Padrick got into the swing of things, I think we both began to see what a blessing this new job was, not just for him, but for me as well. We'd already been working with the Youth at church, but now we had even more access to influence children for good. Even though I had a job of solitude, I started spending a lot of my after hours over at the school, helping Padrick with coaching needs and other special projects he became involved in. I think being around the kids all day kept Padrick's mind occupied. They enjoyed being with Coach K, and he enjoyed being with them. Most times if I had a day off in the week, I'd go over to the school just to hang out or help with Padrick's classes. We were both in amazement over God's timing and placement of Padrick's new employment. We had no doubt it was all a part of God's plan to help us both somehow adjust to life without Raven. He assisted us greatly in our efforts to create a new normal, or at least as much of one as possible. It was just what we both needed, especially with the gradual slowing of activity at home. This new job kept us occupied, as it became more evident the key to our survival would be to stay as busy as possible. It was all a part of God's plan.

5

A YEAR OF FIRSTS

Raven's accident was in January, so with it being the first month of a new year, we had a fresh start to all of the "first" without her to endure. I've heard so many people comment on timing and how losing a loved one during a holiday season would have to be the worst. My response to that hopefully reels in reality with the question, "Is there any good time of the year to lose someone we love?" Could there be a day, a month or a year less painful, leaving you a little less heartbroken? The hole it leaves in your heart is the same size no matter when, and every season after is never the same. Nothing else will ever be as good or as joyful as it once was, because from that moment on, everything you do and everywhere you go will be in the absence of your loved one.

Valentine's Day was our first seasonal celebration without Raven. I'd always done something special for Padrick and Raven, cards and candy of course, and sometimes I'd go all out with balloons and streamers just to be festive. I remember one year I got up a little earlier than usual so that I could decorate the living room and kitchen to surprise Padrick and

Raven. I'd bought the perfect Valentine's Day balloons; they were heart shaped and everything. As I put the first one in my mouth in an attempt to quietly blow it up, it burst right in my face, a piece of it hitting me in the eye. It was pretty painful, not to mention the fact that it woke Padrick and Raven up. My efforts to surprise them turned into a long eye watering day for me. I had a nice blood blister on my eyeball which gave me something to explain for the next few days, it was a good conversation starter.

After Ravens accident, the way I'd always done things for special occasions drastically changed. I can remember being with Padrick at Wal-Mart one day soon after and seeing all the Valentine's Day decorations and having absolutely no interest in participating. I could see that life was going on all around us, and all we could feel was emptiness and pain. Padrick and I were like 2 lost souls without Raven. Just getting up in the mornings and going through the day took all we had and more. The grief we felt drained up physically, mentally, and spiritually, so celebrating anything special became more burdensome to us than joyful, because now everything we did had to be done without Raven to share in it.

After Valentine's Day came our first Easter, which of course reminded me of the hope we have of seeing Raven again. For that I will be eternally grateful, even though at the time I struggled to reflect any spirit of thankfulness in the day. My heart was so broken that it was hard for me to show any gratitude towards God at all. I just couldn't understand why He took Raven away from us, and I was holding a measure of anger towards Him that I wasn't quite ready to let go of. I just trusted that in time I'd somehow be able to address it with Him one on one. Holding on just seemed to give me a false sense of control, like I had some kind of power over the situation I found myself to be in.

Next, came my first Mother's Day without Raven. As hard as it was, I knew I had to somehow get through it. I didn't go to church that day so as to avoid all of the Mother's Day celebrating. Instead, I spent the morning at home. Padrick cooked breakfast for me and I later just laid on Raven's bed, thinking back on Mother's Day past. I'd run into her room, jump on her bed while she was still sleeping and sing, "Happy Mother's Day to me!" She would open her sleepy eyes, look up at me and say, "Oh know, I have to be nice to you today." We'd both laugh and she'd blow her morning breath in my face, hoping to run me away from her sleeping in a little late. Oh, how I missed the way things once were, and how much I longed for them to be again. For lunch that day, Padrick took me to Smithfield's Chicken and BBQ in Jacksonville. On the way back, we stopped by Raven's accident site and put a wooden cross in the ground. We wrote on it and left some plastic roses there. It was a hard, hard day. To my surprise later that evening, many of Raven's friends came over to visit. I was showered with cards and gifts, and I was very appreciative. Company was just what I needed, the company of Raven's friends. Seeing I'd not been forgotten gave my broken heart a reason to smile. It didn't make things any easier, but it did make it a little more bearable. I didn't have my Rae, but I did have those closest to her. It was almost like she'd put a request in to them from Heaven, and they were more than willing to do all they could to help carry me through what they knew would be a painful day.

Raven's accident site Memorial

Father's Day was a lot different. I remember getting up to fix Padrick breakfast like me and Raven always did on his special day. I'd placed a picture of Raven at the table where she normally would have sat, and all Padrick could do was cry. My heart just broke for him. That afternoon he had very few visitors, not as many as I'd had for Mother's Day. I guess people don't really consider so much the pain a father experiences in losing a child. They hurt too; they too lost a child. Men may grieve differently than women, but that doesn't make their level of loss any less. Padrick has his moments too, they're just somewhat restrained. The outward expressions of the grief he feels in losing Raven comes in waves just like mine. I can always tell if he's having a hard day. It's a whole different world behind closed doors. The masks come off and the bottled emotion is free to unload, no stares, no whispers, and no judgement. It's almost like walking in our house from the backdoor brings a sweet release, a disengagement that allows us to stop pretending we're ok. As the world around us continues to move on, we're free to stop "running the plastics," even if only for a few hours. There's no obligation to withhold our feelings to spare uncomfortable or awkward situations. That alone can be so freeing.

Memorial Day and the 4th of July came and went, and there we were to face Raven's 17th Birthday without her. Six days prior was my 38th. We actually spent my Birthday at Caswell with the Youth from our church. A week of summer camp away from home with a load of teenagers was just what I'd needed, especially with it being my first Birthday without Raven. It didn't fill the gap, but it did keep me very busy and occupied. A few days prior, a good friend arranged a surprise Birthday party for me at our church with family and friends. For that I was very thankful. She'd gone above and beyond to make sure that my Birthday was as good as it could possibly be.

Tuesday, August 10, 2010 we had a Birthday Cookout Celebration at our house for Raven. A total of 102 people came out to help us celebrate what would have been Raven's 17th Birthday. The love and support we received that day was beyond measure. We went all out with decorations and food. The entire day was all about Raven "For Raven." One particular gift given to us that day that really stood out was a special memory jar that Padrick's sister Debra made for us. In it was a pad of paper and pen, and all who attended Raven's party that day were encouraged to share a precious memory they had of her. Padrick and I enjoyed reading over each and every one that was written later after the cookout was over that day. We'd

Raven's "Happy Birthday" Memorial Banner

ended the celebration by gathering around Raven's grave and singing "Happy Birthday" to her. We felt we'd done our best to make the day as good as it could be, as bearable as we possibly could, and we were more than thankful for all of our family and friends that showed up to support us on what was a hard day for us both.

In surviving Raven's Birthday, we still had the fall season to get through. School would be starting back, but without Raven. It would have been her senior year of High School, another milestone taken from us. October has always been my favorite month of the year. I love to see the leaves change colors, feel the weather cool down, and buy what I consider my share of pumpkins and mums to decorate around the house with. As a mother, I've always felt it was my duty and pleasure to keep our home in step with every season. I wanted Raven's childhood and teen years to hold memories of a home that brought joy to each new season, so I tried to make it feel as festive as I could. For some reason it just made the seasons come to life even more. It made our house feel like a home.

Fall church events were always anticipated, the Hobo Supper, the Annual Fish Fry and Thanksgiving breakfast. These were all things we enjoyed as a family, but now we found ourselves forced into creating that new normal. Without Raven, nothing was the same. Nothing held the excitement it once did. Losing Raven took the joy out of everything. Our first Thanksgiving without her was so hard. I didn't get off work till later than usual. Around 4pm Padrick, myself and a few of our family members went out to Raven's accident site where we left a cup of cream corn which was always her favorite, 2 pumpkins and some mums. Afterwards me and Padrick went out to Raven's grave. I left a card for her there. We later went over to my parent's house for some leftover Thanksgiving dinner. Things were different, nothing as it had been years prior. We did the best we could to get through the day. It was teary and sad, but we made it.

After Thanksgiving we had Christmas to endure. I'd already determined in my mind that I wasn't going to do any decorating. What was the point? I had absolutely no desire to put up a tree, buy gifts, nothing! My grief in losing Raven had stripped away my reason for wanting to do anything. Padrick had never really helped me to decorate any in the past, but Raven sure did. She loved Christmas and everything about it. I did too when she was here. I'd discussed my plans not to decorate with Padrick, and to my surprise he was in total disagreement. He informed me that choosing to do nothing at all would only make getting through Christmas even harder. He encouraged me to do a little something, or at least as much as I felt that I could. He assured me that doing so would be much better than doing nothing at all, so I took his advice. I put the little Christmas tree I usually decorated for Raven's bedroom on the washstand in the living room, and I hung a wreath on the front door. There were a couple of things that Padrick and I did together to make Raven as much a part of Christmas that year as we could. We had a Christmas themed memorial banner made for Raven to put up in our front yard, and lighted mental yard picks strung with clear and red lights. We knew a man close by who made Christmas yard ornamentals with lights, and he was more than happy to help us out. I gave him a design idea that I'd drawn up, and his creation fit it to a tee. It read <3URAE, and it was perfect. I still use the banner and the yard picks every year at Christmas. Doing so doesn't make Christmas without Raven any easier, but by doing these things in her memory, they provide ways of making her a part of the season while helping to keep her memory alive.

"Love You Rae" Memorial Lights

Christmas Eve morning my parents always had a big breakfast at their house for family and friends, even people from the community would come to be a part of it. Ironically, the year prior, my mama had announced that it would be their last breakfast. It had just gotten so big that it was beginning to become more than they were prepared to handle. I've always had to work, but I do always manage to get a load going by long enough to stop and eat. I never stay long, but long enough to enjoy a little fellowship with family and friends. Sometimes Padrick and Raven would get there about the same time, or just a little before me. Who knew that would be our last Christmas Eve breakfast at my parents with Raven? God knew, and He'd prepared long beforehand. We didn't have the "big breakfast" that following year, just family. I remember stopping by on the truck and crying uncontrollably as I ate breakfast that morning without Raven. It was breathtaking, but not in a good way. No one said a word to me, they just let the tears flow. I did my best to dry them up before I headed back out that day. I'll never forget it. I'll never forget the feeling of not having Raven there with us and knowing it would be that way from then on out. I miss her so much, we all do, but we carry on. It never gets any easier, but we keep moving forward. Today my parents have continued on with their Christmas Eve Breakfast, but mostly just for family since the year of Raven's accident.

Christmas Eve night had always been about getting together with family and keeping up family traditions, but with Raven not here to participate, all of that changed. Our usual flow of festivities to attend no longer held the anticipation they once did. If Raven couldn't be a part of it, we had no desire to contribute. Her absence took all the joy out of it. We usually would go to my mama's brother's house, but I just couldn't that year. Instead, Padrick's sister had a get-to-gather at her house. It was a first, something different, something outside of what we'd always done in the past. After supper at Debra's house that evening, Padrick's family had a surprise candlelight memorial over at Raven's grave. We all sang Silent Night, and his nephew Grant read a special poem. I spoke a few words and so did Padrick, then my daddy prayed. It was a nice thing they'd planned. Raven was remembered, and to me that made it a precious gathering of family and friends in her memory, something I truly appreciated and was very thankful for.

Christmas morning, we went over to my parent's house for breakfast. We'd usually go there to open gifts, then walk over to my grandparents for breakfast and to open more gifts. This time we did it all at my parent's house. It was sad, a first without Raven. It was different, and none of us could even pretend for even a moment that it wasn't. When we left there, we went home to get ourselves ready and prepare for Round 2 of our stops for family gatherings. Before heading off to Padrick's mama's house, we went to visit his daddy's grave and 2 others of some of our friend's children who too had passed away. Visiting Raven's grave again afterwards, I left a jelly biscuit, something I'd promised her in my mind that I'd do. She always loved her jelly biscuits. I miss that too.

After Christmas, Padrick and I had January to face. The 24th would make a year since Raven's accident, and we planned a big 1 Year Memorial for her to be held at our church. That morning after breakfast at Padrick's aunt's restaurant, we drove over to the pharmacy to have some bows made for Raven's Adopt-A-Highway signs. We had lunch later at Raven's favorite place, The Del Rio, then it was back to the church for an afternoon of getting ready. A lot of

Raven's grave site

time and effort went into preparing for Raven's 1-year anniversary. Of course, I had a memorial ad in the paper for her (and have every year since on her Birthday and Anniversary.) We held a big gathering at our church that evening. There were about 250 people who attended. The service went well. I spoke and sang and shared stories of Raven's childhood and teen years. I had Mrs. Lauri Gray, one of our church piano players to play a song from Raven's old piano book. It was one she loved playing back when she was in elementary school. My mama sang a song she used to sing with Raven when she was little, "Hallelujah Anyhow." It was a wonderful celebration of Raven's past. Padrick and I were so touched by the support we received from our family and friends. So many of Raven's classmates were there, even her teammates and coach Mark Lane from the East Duplin Girls Varsity Basketball Team.

At the end of the service that night, Padrick came up and read a devotion from our Open Windows devotional. He shared the ABC's of salvation and opened up the alter for any who desired to give their lives to Jesus that night. My final words were, "Make sure your heart is ready, tomorrow is not a promise." Lots of kids came up to the alter, and our Pastor along with a visiting Pastor, Mr. Tim Rouse, (he baptized Raven) walked up and assisted those who came forward. It was such a blessing to see just how many lives Raven's life and death had touched. My heart is so full to know that so many came to know the Lord through her tragedy, through our greatest loss. It leads me to really believe that good can come from bad. So many times, that's much easier said than seen. I see it now, and I know it for a fact to hold truth. Through our pain, God is glorified.

6

The Five Stages of Grief

Yes, there are 5 stages of grief, I've read up, researched and experienced all but one at this point in the game. Denial holds the number one slot, and for good reason. It's an action word defined, "to declare something to be untrue." It appears to come naturally in the loss of a loved one. I'd say even more so when the loss is sudden and unexpected as Raven's death was. We had no warning or "season of preparation." Life as we knew it was changed in an instant. We went from a happy family of 3 to what felt like stolen joy. Our minds literally could barely process what we saw the evening of January 24, 2010, as our only child lay lifeless on the shoulder of a ditch a good mile or so back in the woods of a hunting club, we were unfamiliar with. Is this what God had planned for us? For Raven? There must have been some kind of mistake. Raven had plans for a bright future. She was only a junior in high school, looking so forward to the start of soccer season and her very first prom. Why? Why did this have to happen?

The first few days were filled with questions. The "what

ifs" took over our minds, overflowing them with doubts and regrets. If only we'd done this or that differently, if only Raven had been here and not there. What went wrong? We had so many questions, mostly ones that I wanted answers to. Padrick said having them wouldn't change the outcome, but I still wanted to know every single detail of what happened that day. I figured that somehow in knowing, I could magically rewind the events of that day, change everything up, and Raven would still be here. All I really wanted to do what fix it and bring her back. I climbed up into the raft of denial and pretended with each new day that it was all just a bad dream, and that I would soon wake up from the pain. That was much easier than admitting to myself that Raven was gone from this life, and that she wasn't coming back no matter what I did.

Sometime after Raven's accident, Padrick told me of several episodes he had prior to. Episodes of overwhelming grief that drew him into dark places of sadness and helplessness. Thinking back to those moments, he believes that it was God speaking to him, preparing him in some way for Raven's death. A few weeks prior, he said he'd asked Raven if she was ready if anything were to happen to her, and she said that she was. He asked a second time, and again she assured him that she was. He has so many times looked back and wondered how he didn't realize that it was God speaking to him in those moments of overwhelming, unexplained grief. It upsets him to see how he failed to make that connection. How could he have known then? How could knowing have made a difference?

After months of living in denial, I slowly began to see that pretending Raven was coming back was no longer an option for me. Waking up every day and looking across the hallway into her bedroom was confirmation of that. Her dirty laundry no longer piled up in the clothesbasket, and she never answered when I called her phone. The house was just quiet and still. The sounds of a teenage daughter no longer filled our home. The denial I had experienced slowly began to transition into stage 2 of the grieving process, that being anger, an anger I tried desperately to suppress in the presence of others. Not even Padrick has seen the full measure of anger in me over losing Raven. It's in my alone time that I allow it to escape, and even then, I struggle to control the measure of my release. I can remember one day being home alone in the shower, and just wanting to scream and shout. So much came out of me that day that I literally lost my breath and feared I'd choke to death. It took me a while to regain and recover. I honestly believe that if the entirety of our grief came on us all at once that it would kill us, and that's why God only allows us to receive it in limited waves. Too much at a time would take us to a place of no return. He gives us what we need to get through, and how we choose to use it is what keeps us accountable. He understands our human nature, however, we have to bring ourselves to an understanding that His will always overrides ours, no matter what we think we can change on our own. We are in control of nothing, only how we react to what happens in our lives and to those we love.

One day I was at work in my truck going down the road, coming back from a farm. I was angry and crying, I was missing my Raven. I screamed out to God in anger, and I said to Him, "You can't possibly know how hard this is for me, you've never been a mother!" It was at that very moment

God spoke directly to me. He said in a loud yet sympathetic way, "I created you, I know everything about you, and I lost my only child for you so that you could have eternity in Heaven with yours!" The tears just kicked into overdrive for me as God reminded me of the sacrifice of His Son Jesus on the cross, and because of that I will see Raven again. I can live with that hope, and I am so thankful. Although I continue to battle occasional waves of anger, when they hit, I think back to that day, and God slowly calms my spirit, reminding me of the time we had with Raven and all that we have to look forward to with her in Heaven.

The third stage of grief is one that I'd say was most shorted lived for me. Bargaining, it was more of a mental thing. With all the alone time I had at work, it was there that I tried so hard to rewrite the outcome of Raven's accident. I'd spend hours every day playing things over and over in my mind, wishing to somehow change it all, and convincing myself that it was even possible. When I finally opened my eyes to the fact that nothing was changing, no matter how much I willed it to, I gave up. Time was passing and Raven was not coming back. She was gone, and there was absolutely nothing we could do to recover the life we had with her. The world was continuing to turn without her, no matter how hard I'd dug my heels in the ground to stop it. Life for everyone else was moving on with or without Raven, and somehow, I had to find the strength in myself to pick up all the pieces of my broken heart and glue them back together. As wounded as I was, I knew my survival was dependent on that. I had no choice but to play the cards God had dealt, so keeping my mental state strong became a top priority for me. Even to this day I continually say to myself, "Focus, stay focused!" God's not a deal maker, and he doesn't owe me a thing.

Depression, it's the 4th stage of grief, and one that will wear you down to the wire if you let it. For me, it's been a daily battle to ward it off, especially because of the fact that I carry so much alone time in my job. It's true what we feed grows, and it's more than obvious that what we stare dies. Everything we expose ourselves to contribute to our thought process in some way. The movies we watch, the music we listen to, the books we read, everything! Even the people we spend time with, family, friends, coworkers, they all influence our thinking in some way. I believe it's very important to self-evaluate during our exposure to people and things in our lives. Do they build us up, or do they tear us down? Grief already takes so much of a toll on our mental state, so why contribute to making it any harder than it already is? I've learned that we have to be intentional about what we allow our eyes to see and our ears to hear. Know who helps and who hurts. Some days are manageable, and then there are days the glue starts to lose its hold, and even the slightest negative words can send you spiraling back down into the darkness you work so hard to stay away from. Once you fall down a notch, you have to work twice as hard to get back to where you were and staying there requires you to engage in a daily mental battle. Your survival is dependent on your choice to fight with everything you have, weakness is not optional.

There have surely been days that I find myself physically and mentally spent from grief. Refueling comes with a determination to stay connected to the source of my strength, and that is the good Lord above. I can't stress enough of how important it is to stay involved in church. The fellowship of my family of believers has contributed greatly to my stability. Daily prayer, Bible reading, devotions, anything that keeps me rooted in my faith has been and continues to be essential to overcoming any onsets of depression. Keeping light in my life keeps my head above water and focusing on what's eternal over the temporary keeps me sane.

Acceptance is the last of the 5 stages of grief, and it is the one my heart just refuses to welcome. I'm not sure that I will ever truly accept that it was God's will to take Raven at 16 years old, even as we continue to live out our days in her absence. At this point, it has been just over 9 years, and I still can't believe it. I still struggle in each and every day. I love the Lord, and I trust Him completely, but I'll never be alright with His choice to take away my only child. For me, to say I accept it is to say I'm good with it, and I'll never be good with it. We have no choice but to live out the rest of our lives here without Raven, but choosing to find that acceptable is not on my agenda at all. Maybe in years to come if I'm still here, I'll finally find a peace about it, but I just haven't gotten there yet. I certainly can't deny that she's gone, but I can still dream. I can still let her memory live on through me. That's something I'll choose to do every day for as long as I have breath. Keeping Raven's memory alive helps me to feel that in some way, she's still here. It's a release and a means of survival. I don't ever want the world to forget about Raven. I know I never will.

7

THE NEED TO READ

I've never been a big reader, Raven wasn't either. I can remember when she was in Elementary School. She had to read a certain number of books every so many weeks and then be tested on each one. It was all a part of an Accelerated Reading Program, and for her it was torture. Reading was just not her thing, and her dislike for it became a nightly chore for me. The only way she could manage to get through her assigned reading journey was to drag me in it with her. Like every mother, I wanted Raven to be successful in school, but I learned fairly quick that you can't make someone who hates to read love it. It started out with making her read aloud while I jotted down questions to ask after every chapter. It was a slow, long drawn out process, but I could see improvements along the way. It was helping her tremendously, but also soaking up way too much time. Our evenings were spent mostly reading on top of other homework assignments she had. To speed things up a little, I decided I'd take turns reading with her, she'd read a chapter, then I'd read one. I wrote down potential test questions for each one we read, and like before, I'd ask her to answer every single one aloud to make sure she was paying attention. It seemed she enjoyed the Ramona Quimby books by Beverly Clearly best, so we read as many of those as we could get our hands on. Believe it or not, I actually liked the Ramona books too, they were pretty entertaining and covered real life situations. Ramona became a part of our family, or at least that's how it felt. She was no longer just a character in a book, she was a friend to Raven and me. We got to know her on a personal level. Ha! As challenging as getting your child through elementary school can be, I sure miss those days with Raven. I'd go back in a heartbeat if I could.

Aside from those years of reading with Raven, I've never really been big on reading books either. I guess it's because I find myself too busy with other things in life. I'm not one to sit still for long periods of time; I like to be on the move. I can make a piddle session out of most anything, especially outside. I love being outdoors on a pretty, sunny day. You'd sure never find me lounging around with a book in my hands. That's just too quiet and too still for me.

After Raven's accident, I was drawn to books about death and Heaven. I was broken to the core and desperately searching for something tangible to keep me afloat. I knew I had the Bible, but I wanted something identifiable to today's terms. I knew God would carry me in my grief, but I needed to see what he'd done for others in my shoes, how others managed in the loss of a child. I needed some kind of confirmation that I would make it written out on paper from the experience of another grieving parent, especially a mother, and I got that through many of the books I've read. I confess, some books only contributed to my ongoing depression, but others helped set my feet back on solid ground. Padrick was always the first to recognize any downward spiral in my progress, and so he would search out books that he felt would help me along, all the while struggling himself. He was never drawn to read them personally, but he did seem to show a great interest in hearing my feedback of the books he bought for me.

Sometimes a book would just show up at just the perfect time. It was like God had some specific reads in mind, especially for me. I can remember on one occasion, sitting at the dentist office in the waiting room with Padrick. We were both scheduled for a cleaning that day as we usually go together. I was looking through a magazine and saw an advertisement for a book I'd recently heard about and wanted to eventually get. It was a book written by Mary Beth Chapman titled, "Choosing to See." The book was about the tragic loss of her daughter Maria. I showed the magazine article to Padrick and told him how much I really wanted that book, and how I intended on soon getting a copy. Later on, after our dental appointments were done, we headed back home and stopped to check the mail over at the post office on the way. I got out to go inside and was surprised to see that we'd gotten a package. I opened it up to find a copy of the book, "Choosing to See," the same book I'd just earlier told Padrick that I'd been wanting to get. Wow! How awesome is that? My cousin Melissa had sent it to me, and she'd written a special note to me inside the cover. Now that was a "God Thing." The timing of it all still blows me away.

I've always heard it said that God is never early and never late, He's right on time. I believe that with all of my heart. I remember another book I'd been wanting to read. It was about Heaven and a little boy who'd died and gone there for a visit. It was titled, "Heaven Is for Real," and it gave in detail this little boy's experience in Heaven. Wouldn't you know that after some conversation with Padrick about it, we came home one evening to find a copy of it left on our back porch from our friend Tina. Wow, another "God Thing!" What are the chances of that happening? None, there are no chances when it comes to God's timing, it's all just a part of what He already had planned, coming to be. There's a good chance of something happening if you truly believe, and I believe!

Romans 8:28 tells us that in all things God works for the good of those who love him who have been called according to His purpose. I believe in God, and I believe He's working for my good. With all the books I've read so far, I do have one that I consider to be my most favorite, and that book is Appointments with Heaven by Dr. Reggie Anderson with Jennifer Schuchmann. It's just awesome, and ironically the author happens to be good friends with Steven and Mary Beth Chapman. I have a friend who enjoys reading in general, so I recommended this book to her, and she too agreed of what an awesome read it was. When we find something that offers encouragement and builds our faith, I think it's important to share that with others. Once Padrick and I came home to a water disaster that was the result of what I'll call a mix of minor distraction and plain forgetfulness on Padrick's part. Ha! The next day, our insurance company sent Servpro to our house to take out the wet flooring and set up fans and humidifiers. For the next few days, our house was a disaster area. When Servpro came back to pick up their equipment, Padrick and I got a chance to really met the guys who'd done the clean-up job. They'd obviously noticed the many memorials in our home for Raven during their time there, and one of them asked us what happened to her. We shared the story of Raven's death and found that he and his wife too had lost a child, a baby. He told us that his wife was really struggling and how hard it had been on them both. I shared of the comfort I found in so many of the books I'd read, and I offered to give them one in particular that identified with their loss personally. He accepted the offer, and I gave him the book that had been given to me. I realized that the chances of having the book returned were slim, but I was ok to let it go if it could in anyway help someone else as it had helped me. Could it have been that our home water disaster was ordained by God to get this particular man to our house for this particular book for his wife? Yes, I think so. I don't think it was by accident that we came to meet each other at such a time. I believe God was in it. It was an opportunity for us to help someone else through words of encouragement and a book that related to his situation of loss. That night after our Family Scripture Time, Padrick and I prayed over that man and his wife, trusting and believing that God would carry them just as he continues to carry us in and out of each new day. He is our hope and our peace, the key to surviving in the loss of Raven.

8

OTHER PEOPLE'S CHILDREN

When you lose a child, especially an only child, you find yourself at the mercy of sharing in the lives of other people's children. Unless you're a hermit who never intends to venture out into the world again, you painfully feed off the energy that continues on for other families with children the age your child lived to be. At least that's the case for me personally.

Prior to Raven's accident, I was already working with the Youth in our church, a group Raven was very active in and one I continue to lead. We have kids that range from grades 7 to 12, so I have seen many come and go over the years, and each one holds a special place in my heart. I admit, it's hard watching them all grow up and become young adults, wishing so much to have seen that happen for Raven. I'm glad for them, but at the same time sad for Padrick and myself. For us Raven will forever be 16, midway into her junior year of high school, and looking so forward to her first prom. We still have the money she was saving to buy the dress she wanted so much to have, one she never got the chance to buy.

March of 2010 was our upcoming Youth Sunday at church. With a church ski trip planned a few weeks prior, we had a lot going on with preparation and getting things organized for both. To everyone's surprise, Raven had volunteered to sing a special with Devan, another of our Youth. He'd already planned to sing, but he was more than happy to have Raven offer to sing along with him. I never imagined I'd end up singing in her place that day, who knew? Things were going really well. I'd prayed over this new year, expecting God to really bless. With the news of Raven's friend Justin being declared cancer free on the 13th of January, things were already off to an awesome start. Justin was a year ahead of Raven in school. Back in their Jr. High days they were boyfriend and girlfriend for a season, but they remained friends even after. Halfway into Justin's Jr. year of High School, he found out that he had cancer in one of his femur bones. Of course, Raven, Padrick and I were greatly concerned as we all thought so much of Justin and his family. We kept in close contact, and through a hard year of treatments, surgery and continuous prayers, Justin overcame his battle with cancer. He has and continues to be there for Padrick and I in the loss of Raven. He and his sister Jayne have been such a blessing to us over the years.

I have to say first and foremost, staying active in church has been very instrumental in surviving our losing Raven. Working with the Youth has in many ways kept Padrick and myself afloat. We never really even skipped a beat in preparing for our Youth Sunday that March, but we did struggle greatly in Raven's absence. Through lots of tears, hugs and prayers, we pressed on in her memory. That day we not only remembered Raven, but other Youth we'd lost as well, Kameron, Dustin and Derick. After the service we had a big dinner in the fellowship hall and later gathered outside over at our church cemetery to bury Raven's ashes. All that I could think in that moment was, "How did we get here?" I knew in my heart that Padrick and I were going to need those kids to help us. Even though Raven was gone, we knew God still had work for us to do. He's obviously not finished with us yet, and even now years later, we do our best to stay focused and continue on in God's plan for our lives. We carry Raven's memory along with us every step of the way.

There is a particular scripture in the Bible I think of often as I look back on the waves of support Padrick and I have had over the years. It comes from Ecclesiastes Chapter 3:1-8. When I read it to myself, it reminds me of just how seasonal the things in this life are. Everything in life as we know it in this world is limited and controlled by time. Everything here comes with a date of expiration. It's like a good friend always says, "This too shall pass." That includes the good and the bad, nothing here will last forever. Immediately following Raven's accident, Padrick and I found ourselves overwhelmed with support, and now 9 years later, it's rare to even hear the mention of her name outside of our own conversations of her.

I've learned over the passing of time that those who've gone on before us will be as remembered as we make the effort for them to be. As Raven's mother, I go above and beyond to make sure that she is never forgotten, but I know some mothers who don't even so much as leave a fresh flower on the graves of their children, not even for Birthdays or Anniversaries. I don't understand that, and I probably never will. As far as I see it, as long as I have breath, mental capability and mobility, efforts will be made on my part to keep Raven's memory alive. What reason have I to be offended or upset by the neglect and lack of attentiveness towards her from others, if I as her mother sit back and do nothing? It's like a friend of mine said recently, "If I do nothing, who else will?" Now I realize that everyone grieves differently, and that my thoughts and ideas aren't shared by all, but hey, they contribute to my survival, so I'll continue to do what I know is best for me.

Getting back to the topic of seasonal things and other people's children, I can surely testify that time changes things. Most of the people who were, no longer are. In saying that, I can tell you one thing that is certain, God provides! He puts certain people in our lives, just the right ones at just the right times. He knows when to bring them in and how long to keep them there. I can't help but consider Padrick's students, they're all with him for a season, they come, they grow, and they go. Some stay connected in some manner, while others are rarely to be seen again. I believe God had purposed each for a season in our lives and theirs. We hold each other close, even if only for a few short years, knowing all the while that the passing of time will eventually take us or them in different directions. In my mind, I've determined not to allow this simple fact to create any long-lasting sadness in my heart. I just remind myself of what we've been through and continue to struggle with. If we can continue to breathe and survive in the loss of our only child, surly we can manage to stay afloat in the transition of someone else's child from High School to becoming a young adult. We've witnessed continued church connection for some, and a total world jump for others. Either way, a seed was planted, and prayers are lifted on their behalf. I feel we've done our best to minister and counsel each with as much passion as we did for Raven, not wanting any to perish in a sea of bad choices from worldly influences. We've been constant to remind them of how tomorrow is promised to none, and we have provided plenty of examples from within our own church family to share. I think it's safe to say that Padrick and I have loved them as our own. We've both been so blessed to have each one be a part of our lives if only for a short time. We've learned that it is possible to find some measure of joy in loss through the fellowship and friendship of other people and their children. They can never replace what we lost in Raven, but they do give us purpose while we're here, and for that we are truly thankful.

9

OUR NEW NORMAL

A new normal, three words that directly address change, something I've never been a welcome mat for, especially when that change involves the death of a loved one. I've lost grandparents, great aunts and uncles, many of whom I'd expect to "go on" before me, but what could ever be normal about losing a child? Nothing! Parents aren't supposed to outlive their children, it's just not the natural order of things, and those of us who have can never express in words the depth of pain associated in the loss of a child. It completely changes your view of the world in every way possible. It robs the joy of your heart like nothing else can, and it strips you down to the wire, leaving you no choice but to force even the next breath. It feels like your lungs have lost the ability to function, and you have to remind yourself mentally to inhale and exhale.

I'll never forget Padrick and I going to visit a friend and his wife who had lost their 6-year -old son in an accident the day prior. Walking up to the front porch of their home, we saw him standing there in tears. As Padrick approached him, he reached out to hug him and said something I'll never forget, "I didn't know that ya'll hurt this bad." I went inside to find his wife in tears sitting on their couch. I hugged her and held her for a minute. She said to me, "I feel like I can't breathe." Those are thoughts and feelings you come to know well when you suddenly lose a huge chunk of your life. There's no time to prepare your heart for the loss. It's like you go from life as normal to total devastation and shock, and I'm sad to say that feeling lingers long after the initial play out. I'm convinced that you never truly recover from the loss. You're forced into a new normal and a new way of life that will never again be as it once was before. You can kick and stomp and fight against it with all you've got, but things will be different from now on, and there's not one thing you can do about it. I've come to learn over the passing of time that you can choose to be mad about it and live your life in a constant state of anger and rage, or you can choose to lace up your boots and navigate through your journey of grief in hope and expectation, trusting God that your "morning will come." The joy we lost in death will be restored in his timing, we just have to believe that, it's vital to our survival.

I've come to know grief on an extremely personal level since the loss of Raven, and so far, my experience has proven to hold no expiration date. I read a book once that stated the 5-year mark to hold somewhat of a "getting over it" point, but for me, after 5 years, the pain still exists. I still wake up and get that morning punch in the stomach. I continue to endure those random waves of nausea as I live in this new normal. A lump in the throat at the onset of tears still cautions me to keep a tissue on hand for every occasion.

Memories of Raven flood my mind on a daily basis. I will never "get used to or get over it." I'll never overcome the emptiness living life in her absence brings. Every day that I'm here is another day that she won't be, but every day that passes brings me one day closer to being where she is. I command myself to look at it that way. It's what keeps me focused during those times of extreme weakness. Somedays I manage my grief like a beast, and other days it overtakes me to the point of just wanting to throw in the towel. If I'm having a good day, I milk every second out of it because I know bad days are coming. It's true how things around us contribute to our thoughts and actions, the music we listen to, the movies and shows we watch, the company we keep. They all in some way help, hurt or hinder our grief journey. It's good to surround ourselves with positive things and encouraging people, keeping ourselves mindful of the fact that what we invest our time and energy in will feed our thoughts and actions. It's important to intentionally avoid anything or anyone that can potentially drag you down. I continue to be amazed at how some people thrive in the weaknesses of others. For some reason they seek out opportunities to offer advice to you on topics they have no real insight on. They feel entitled to evaluate your experience and judge your progress in the measurements of their standards. They honestly think they know where you should be in your grief journey by a certain point, and they are clueless of how little they can really identify with your loss. Although they can sympathize immediately following, their lives go back to normal, so they automatically assume yours has too. Just say what they need to hear and pray it never happens to them. Your life in this world has been forever changed, and they will never really understand what it's like for you personally. You can try to explain and describe it, but be warned, you're wasting your breath.

In doing life different, I think we must keep in mind first that God still has us here for a reason. I have to remind myself of that daily. Our purpose in life has not yet been fulfilled, even if our desire to contribute to the world we live in has. This "new normal thing" involves a lot of unwanted and unwelcomed change. It also requires a lot of understanding from family and friends. They may not transition smoothly, but they have to be willing to try a new way when it comes to traditions and the old way of doing things. For example, our first Christmas without Raven was brutal. Nothing was as it had been in years prior and being around family was not on my radar at all. I'd say by now that the dust has settled as far as what's expected when it comes to holidays and other special occasions, but it still never feels right without Raven. Her presence and participation continue to be missed. I still find myself scanning the room for her whereabouts, longing to catch a glimpse of her interacting with everyone, and enjoying the fellowship of family and friends. Raven was all about family get-to-gathers. She had such a spirit about her, she could light up the room with her outgoing personality and contagious laughter. Her absence is felt at every gathering, but we do our best to muster through and make the most of it, all the while carrying her memory close in our hearts and minds. She's gone, but she'll NEVER, ever be forgotten.

When I think about life "going on" without Raven, I have to admit it stirs a spirit of anger in me, because on Sunday January 24th 2010 at 4:59pm, our world stopped turning. Padrick and I had to figure out among ourselves, where do we go from here? We're still asking ourselves that question, almost on a daily basis. It literally feels like you've been pushed outside of the circle of life, because order has been shaken out of what was expected, never to be as it once was again.

Our new normal for Family Portraits

As the years continue to pass by, the mirror gives a strong testament of the fact that we aren't getting any younger. Our eyes are not as strong as they once were, our bodies are now starting to carry the wear and tear of time, proving to us both that we can't push them quite as hard as we used to. I've always said that aging is God's reminder to us that everything in this life is temporary. Unless we die young, we're all going to see old age eventually, and that is a normal part of life that many grow to be. Those who don't will be forever young in our minds. That's what Raven will be in our minds, forever young, always a Sweet 16. As I write this, we are just coming out of what would have been her 26th Birthday. This year in her memory, we hosted a Community Soup Kitchen at our church. We served chili, vegetable beef soup, and chicken noodle soup. We added 2 of Raven's favorite sandwiches to the mix, grilled chesses and peanut butter and jellies. We also bought gift cards to two of her favorite places to eat, Subway and Bojangles. Those were donated to the people in our area who are helping flood victims recover from last year's Hurricane Florence. We were specific to get 13 of each card to total 26. Doing things like this has become a part of our new normal. We can't buy gifts for Raven anymore, but we can do special things for others in her memory. Somehow by doing so, we manage to keep our focus on something good aside from spending the day wallowing in our grief. It would be so easy to just sit around and allow sorrow and deep sadness to take over, but we choose to be as strong as we possibly can with each passing year, preparing as best we can for all the things we'll have to face again and again in Raven's absence. It never gets easier, but from years past, we've learned to prepare, knowing more so what to expect and how to deal with it. It's our new thing, change we didn't ask for, change we don't like, but change we try hard to adjust to. It's not like we really have any other choice in the matter. What was once normal for us, will never be again.

Memorializing Raven's Heavenly Birthday's Every Year

10

PROTECT THE GOAL

Protect the goal! That was Raven's motto on the soccer field. She played defense and always said, "If the other team scores, it's our fault for letting the ball get that far." She'd never blame the goalie, always those defending it. I can remember her first season of soccer. She was in the 1st Grade and decided she wanted to play, so we signed her up, got her some cute little soccer cleats, socks and chin guards, and she was well on her way. It didn't take long for her to determine that it involved way more running than she'd anticipated, so halfway through, she shared with Padrick and I that she wanted to quit. With what we'd already invested in her short soccer career, quitting was not optional for Raven as far as we were concerned. We wanted her to learn that she would be expected to finish anything she started, and no amount of tears or consistent complaints would sway our decision. We'd never force her to do anything, but we didn't want to raise a quitter either. She learned the hard way and early on to invest some real thought into her choices because follow through was definite where any amount of time and money were spent. She finished out that first season of soccer, and she decided the next year not to play. Several years later, she gave it another chance. This time the running didn't bother her so much. It wasn't long before it became her thing, her favorite sport, her passion. Her first season of rec soccer as a 7th grader brought us to Melvin and Krista Phillips, 2 people who just seemed to water the seed of soccer in Raven's heart. She was challenged to play hard, be respectable and give a hundred percent, nothing less. Melvin, Krista and their children became like family to us all. It wasn't just any soccer team, it was the fellowship of friends, fun times and sweet memories in the making. They didn't just coach, they got to know each player on a personal level. That was huge, and that is why asking them to be a part of Raven's memorial service was so important to Padrick and myself.

Over the years, Raven had been coached by many, but none really knew her like Melvin and Krista. Melvin spoke at Raven's memorial, and he and Krista sang a song together as Krista played the piano. I'd asked a few of Raven's friends to speak, one of whom was with her the day of the accident. Of course, our pastor spoke too. I'd mustered up the courage to speak and sing myself, all the while with my mother up on stage with me on standby. Raven's service was held in the auditorium of the high school she attended. There was no casket, just a black and white photo of Raven and her cat Simba in a frame sitting on a pedestal. It was a selfie she'd taken, one we'd found on her camera just days prior, an unexpected treasure.

The night of Raven's memorial was just mind boggling on so many levels. The sadness and shock of all that had happened was a lesson to everyone there of just how quickly life as we know it can change. Raven's service was on a Wednesday, 3 days after the accident. The Wednesday prior, she had a basketball game at another school nearby, and afterwards she rode back to East Duplin with Padrick to get her truck. He shared with me that as he passed by the memorial of a former classmate of hers across from the school, he'd thought to himself how that could have been Raven. Just a week later, it was.

"Soccer" Raven's favorite sport "Protect the Goal"

I think in life we all at some point play the "what ifs" in our minds. We're aware of the possibilities each new day can bring, but sometimes we tend to stroll through as if any shots fired are sure to miss our targets. We pray for God's protection, expecting and believing, hoping all the while that no fiery furnaces challenge our faith. What do we do in the face of our worst fear when it becomes our reality? If we profess ourselves as Christians, I believe God will sooner or later test us. Do we really trust Him? Do we believe that in all things He has our best interest at heart? As parents, are Padrick and I really expected to find any good associated with the loss of our only child? Yes, yes and yes! As painful as it is, we can continue to move and breathe, but it has to be a choice. We must be intentional about choosing to find a rainbow in the rain. We know where Raven is. She is safe in the arms of God, and as John 10:28-30 says, nothing can snatch her out of His hands. We miss Raven so much, but we live each day knowing we will be with her again someday in Heaven.

In looking back and as we continue to move forward; it is evident that Raven's life and death touched the hearts of so many people. To this day, those we don't really even know come up to us when we're out and about to offer words of sympathy and encouragement. Some who knew Raven personally will share their memories of her, and that always brings some measure of joy to our broken hearts. Staying focused on the eternal is key to our survival. We set our eyes on Heaven, thanking Jesus and knowing that with every passing day we're one step closer to being with Raven again. We run the race wounded, but we run. It's a painful, tear filled process, but our mission is to finish strong in Raven's memory. Our goal is to get from here to where she is, and we'll "protect that goal" with everything we've got. In those moments of deep sadness and on days we struggle most, we hold steady the shields of our faith, knowing that this separation won't last forever.

11

PENNIES FROM RAVEN

Sometime after Raven's accident, a couple of friends of ours took Padrick and I out for a weekend getaway to Myrtle Beach. They too had lost a child several years prior, so they'd found themselves led of God to spend some time consoling us in our loss of Raven. Who better to offer comfort and hope in loss than others who share in your pain? It's received better coming from people who've experienced your loss personally. They understand your degree of suffering like no one else, they know exactly what you're feeling as they remember their own early stages of grief.

I believe it's true what they say about grief, everybody handles it differently. Some people shut down and others strive to survive as best they can. Some seek out the help of support groups, while others slowly disengage from the world. I think either way, the pain associated with the loss grips you like nothing else. The only real escape is pretending it's all a bad dream, but reality settles in eventually, sometimes making you long for sleep so your mind gets some kind of break. I'm so thankful for the people God sends to us to remind us that we're not alone.

Our weekend at Myrtle Beach turned into a celebration of future penny finds for Padrick and I. Our friends Cameron and Sherry had decided to cook a special meal for us on night 2 of our stay. We'd all gone to the grocery store to get what was needed for the dinner, and on our way back to the car, Cameron spotted 2 pennies on the ground in the parking lot. He picked them up, handed one to me and kept one for himself. He said, "These pennies are from Chris and Raven." He told me that every time we find a penny it was from Raven, and that she was letting us know that she's ok, and that she's watching over us. I kept the penny, and held on to that hope, the hope in what he said, anticipating the next "penny find" for Padrick and myself.

In the days, weeks and months to follow, we became like human metal detectors. Even today as we walk around from here to there, our heads face down to the ground in search of pennies, pennies from our precious Raven. Of course, like most everyone else, we've found pennies in the past prior to losing Raven, but none meant as much as they do now. It seems the more desperately we search, the less likely we find any. It's in those moments we least expect, that Raven shows up with a penny in just the right place at just the right time. It's as if she perfectly plans each and every one. Ironically, as I write, today September 3, 2019, I found a penny on the farm path of my last load at work. I was just walking along, getting some steps while unloading, and there it was, Raven! Now, here it is Wednesday, September 4th, 2019, and first thing this morning I find a penny from Raven in the driver break area at work. I'd already found 4 more after yesterday's B & O Farm surprise, so that makes 6 so far in the past 2 days.

For every penny Padrick and I find, I journal of the when's and where's. There's no doubt that I could write a book on just our penny finds alone, but I realize the history in that information would only hold real importance to me and Padrick. There are however many that really stand out, and the stories behind them are nothing short of amazing, as we believe them to be planned of God. If anyone, He surely understands our need for signs of Raven's presence in our lives. Her absence is felt in every fiber of being in our daily lives, so if a penny brings some measure of comfort, we'll continue to find joy in each one we stumble upon.

One morning I was working, and I'd driven up to one of our farms with a gate known to be a challenge to open. I say this because I've personally struggled countless times over the years to get it open myself. It's designed in a way that creates an aggravation for any unwanted, uninvited guests, making any attempt of potential break-ins require real effort. Unfortunately, that includes those of us in feed, live haul and dead haul, who have good reason to get in and out. Anyway, I got out of my truck in the dark with a flashlight, and already prepared myself for something I expected to take several minutes to do. I held my flashlight steady between my chest and chin and started the dreaded process of trying to get the gate open. As I shinned the light down onto the hardest lock ever to open, to my surprise I saw a penny there laying on the ground underneath. The light shinned directly down on it. I smiled, saying to myself, "Raven!" With no real struggle or fight, the key went perfectly into the lock, and in about 2 seconds I had the gate open, Wow! What were the chances of that happening? It just had to be Raven. There's no other explanation. She saw my concern for what had always been a hinderance in the past, and she threw me a bone in penny form. She assisted me by making something that had always been a pain to deal with almost effortless. She saved me time and aggravation, plus distracted me from my fear of being approached by any unseen spiders or snakes. For that I am grateful.

I can remember some time ago the high school Raven attended having a 50-year celebration. Padrick and I went, as we too attended the same school. Classrooms had been set up in honor of each years graduating class, so we made sure to visit ours and what would have been Ravens. To our surprise, a little memorial had been set up for Raven in the room representing the class of 2011, the year she would have graduated. Our hearts were so blessed to see that she had been remembered by her class of students. It wasn't long before we heard an announcement informing those attending the celebration of an assembly to be held in the auditorium. Padrick didn't really want to attend the assembly as he was ready to go, but just before we left, I managed to talk him into one last walk through the lobby where memorabilia from teachers and of classrooms past had been set up to view. I went over to the stairway, stepped up to the first platform, and said to Padrick, "This was the last place that I saw Raven in this school." As I looked down at the floor, there at my feet was a penny, Raven! We'd just been up that very stairway moments prior, and we didn't see any pennies. Wow! Just wow! A few days before her accident, Padrick and I were off from work together. We neither one had given Raven any money for lunch that day, so we drove to the school, and I went inside to call her out of class to give her some money to buy her lunch with. I remember seeing her coming down the stairway and stopping at that last platform on her way down. She saw me standing there at the office and started smiling. Relived that she was not in trouble for anything, she said, "What are you doing here?" I explained, and she quickly put in a Bojangles request. Somehow, I saw that coming, but I didn't mind. In no time Padrick and I were back at school with a box of Chicken Supremes. She came out to retrieve them with a kiss and a big thank you. I'll never forget that day. The penny I found on the platform of that stairway was a sweet reminder of the last memory I have of Raven at her high school. Who knew what the next few days would bring?

One year on Padrick's Birthday, I'd asked for Raven to please leave him a penny. I was specific, almost demanding for it to be that day, and I'd determined in my mind that Raven would deliver. As the day went by, nothing! That afternoon, we stopped by a Wal-Mart to pick up a Birthday cake for Padrick to enjoy later with family. Walking across the parking lot to go inside, I thought to myself, "Raven, where's that penny for your daddy?" We got the cake, came back out to the parking lot, and I shared with Padrick my disappointment in Raven not leaving even the slightest hint of a penny for him. At that point, it was basically all I'd really asked of her that day. That very moment, Padrick and I walked right up on a penny. When I saw it, I practically crumbled and broke into tears. People walking near and around us must have thought I'd tripped and fallen as Padrick reached out to lift me back up. All this emotion stirred over a single penny? Yes, that's how important it was. I guess Raven was testing me, and the wait and anxiety almost cost me a passing grade. She hadn't let me down, I'd just expected it in my time not hers. Maybe that's the mother in me, what she might consider me nagging her this side of Heaven. What better way to get her attention? To repeat is only to remind, that's what I always say.

Ironically, some pennies we find from Raven we are unable to retrieve. More so to be seen, not taken to save. Another trip to Myrtle Beach lead us to a jack pot of pennies. Padrick and I had decided to get-a-way for a weekend at Broadway At the Beach. On what was a beautiful day outside, we walked around, enjoying the scenery. It wasn't long before we found ourselves being somewhat stalked by an orange butterfly. Orange was Raven's favorite color, so this little butterfly sure got our attention. It fluttered all around us, moving away a little at a time as if it wanted us to follow its lead. We kept our eyes fixed on it, and we began moving in the direction it took us. Just minutes later, we were standing right in front of a stingray water fountain, and it was full of shiny pennies. We knew at that point exactly what that little butterfly wanted, the reason behind its efforts to get our attention, it was Raven! We didn't take any of the pennies, we just got ourselves a good gander, and we loved every second of it.

While we were there, walking around, taking in the scenery. We came up to a booth where pictures of letters in sign language were being sold. Oh, the ideas that brought. It took me back to when Raven and I had taken sign language classes at Chinquapin Elementary School. We had the best time ever, we learned so much. While we stood there looking, I imagined to myself how cool it would be to use sign letters in Raven's upcoming church arrangement. Next thing I knew, we were picking out for ourselves an R, N and K. As Padrick and I stood there, waiting to pay, we noticed a penny stuck to one of the boards on the floor at our feet. It was as if it had been unnoticed by whomever glazed the boardwalk, and it could possibly be permanently attached until the eventual wear and tear of foot traffic set it free. We asked the cashier about retrieving it, and we explained our reason behind wanting it so badly. He had no problem with our request, and even made a great effort himself to break it loose for us with a pair of scissors that he just happened to have there with him.

Seeing that penny there was like an approval, confirmation from Raven that using sign letters for her next arrangement was a great idea. I like to think that she planned it that way. The orange butterfly, the stingray water fountain full of pennies, and the booth of photographed hands posing letters in sign language, that was all from Raven. She practically set it up, she all but spoke it to our hearts. To this day that RNK hangs on the wall upstairs in the half-bath of The Bookie Barn. A place expect it'll stay for years to come, good Lord willing.

I could honestly share of penny find stories "till the cows come home" as they always say, but for fear of boring you the reader, I won't. There is however, just one more that Padrick recommended I add to this chapter, so I did. It's too good not to share, so here goes. One day while at work, I had some downtime to fill, so I decided I'd scroll through my Facebook news feed. I came across what was a recently bereaved mother who'd lost her teenage son. His Birthday was approaching, and she was reaching out for ideas on what she could do to make it bearable for herself while at the same time, keeping his memory alive the best way possible. My heart just broke for her, knowing full well how she felt, and I immediately responded, sharing with her special things that she could do for her son, things Padrick and I had done for Raven on her special day. As I wrote in response to this woman whom I didn't know personally, I felt a connection as I realized how we shared a common loss. I knew exactly how hard it was going to be for her to get through her son's Birthday in his absence, it's an empty like no other. I started thinking about Raven as I wrote, "On her Birthday this year, she'll be turning 22." My mind was already racing with ideas, and this woman's request for help just kicked my thoughts into overdrive.

After work that day, I'd ordered Chinese food for supper, so I drove over a short distance away to pick it up after my shift ended. I went inside to pay, and on my way back out to my truck to leave, just a few steps prior, I noticed a penny. I bent down to get it, and there was another, and another and another. I soon had myself a hand full of pennies. I laid them all out in the palm of my hand, and I counted each one to find that there were exactly 22, Wow! How awesome is that? What are the chances of me finding exactly 22 pennies in the same place at the same time? The timing of it all was just amazing, and no doubt planned of God, Raven too of course, and right after my Facebook post to the newly bereaved mother who'd lost her son. Not long after, I purchased an orange picture frame and made a penny project out of my find. Amazingly, I had exactly enough pennies to hot glue down a number 7, Raven's favorite number.

I expect the future to hold many more penny finds for Padrick and myself, and I intend on continuing to journal the story behind each one, no matter how short or long that may be. Some time ago when I was listening to a radio station at work, I heard that soon the manufacturing of pennies will end, and they will no longer be a part of the collection of coins we use today. They were said in so many ways to be useless and unnecessary. I strongly disagree, and for obvious reasons. For Padrick and I they are like breadcrumbs to Heaven, little reminders that Raven is there waiting and watching over us. We will be together again one day, and every penny we find just encourages us to keep pressing on in her memory. We realize we're only a heartbeat and breath away from a much-anticipated sweet reunion. Oh, what a day that will be! Praise God! We can live in the hope He gives through His Son Jesus! Because of his death and resurrection, we know that even though we may weep for now, our joy will come in the morning, Psalm 30:5. We have an eternity to make up for the time we lost in this life with Raven. Hallelujah praise the Lord and thank you Jesus!

22 Birthday Pennies Found Making a Perfect
7 Raven's Favorite Number

These Pennies remind us of our hope in Jesus Christ and that through
His redemptive work we have the assurance of spending Eternity
with Jesus and Raven. Put your trust in Him and ask Him to forgive
your sins and you can have that blessed assurance too! Romans 10:9

REFERENCES

The Holy Bible, NIV Copyright 1973, 1978, 1984 International Bible Society

(Matt. 5:45), (Job 2:7, 14:5), (Jas 4:13-15), (Jer 1:5), (Luke 12:7), (Ps 139:16, 30:5), (Rom 8:28 and 10:9), (John 3:16 and 10:28-30)

MORE ABOUT RAVEN

When you become a parent, your greatest fear is losing your child. When you lose a child, your greatest fear is that the world will "go on" and forget that they were here. Keeping their memory alive becomes almost mission like, or at least that's how I'd define my personal experience. I take advantage of most every opportunity I get to keep Raven's memory afloat in what I sometimes view to be a worldly sea of forgetfulness. I figure I'm her mother, if I don't carry her memory, who will? Although Padrick supports all of my ideas and efforts, I honestly don't see him taking over to the degree that I do in the event I pass before him. I expect he'll continue to carry Raven's memory, but not in a "motherly me" kind of way. I realize that may make him sound somewhat less grieved, but I can tell you that is far from the truth. Men just grieve differently than women do. Padrick misses Raven just as much as I do. That's a fact, I see it every day.

When it comes to sharing an event or even a simple precious memory, social media has served us well. I don't post anything of Raven to fish for sympathy. My intentions are solely to keep her memory alive while also possibly helping other bereaved parents cope in the loss of their children. It surely helps to know you're not alone in what feels like living your worst nightmare. Padrick and I have been counseled and comforted by so many who've walked this road ahead of us, and it's our duty to do the same for those behind us. Not all losses come in the same manner, but they all leave the same hole in your heart, a hole nothing in this world can ever truly fill.

I think that I can safely speak on behalf of others when I say how much it means to us to know that our children have not been forgotten. To hear their name spoken in conversation or see that something has been done in their memory just warms our broken hearts. I love hearing someone else share their memories of Raven, it's music to my ears. Just as I'd mentioned in a previous chapter, on what would have been her 17th Birthday when we received the memory jar from Padrick's sister. What a treasure! Sometimes even now, I just go back and reread the memories that were shared on that special day. What a precious gift the memory jar was, and still is to this day.

When others share their memories of Raven, I can honestly tell if they're interested to hear of any Padrick or myself are willing to share, so I jump at the chance and take advantage of every opportunity. Just saying her name aloud affords me a momentary window of pretending she's still here. I like to speak of her as if she is, and even though reality proves different, she's still very much a part of our lives. We carry her in our hearts every single day. Our memories of her are precious treasures we hold dear.

Sometimes people will just come right out and ask us questions about Raven, and when they do, Padrick and I are more than willing to answer. Because we write on her Facebook wall daily, much of what anyone may want to know can be gathered from there. I do most of those writings. For me, it provides a way to somehow feel as if I'm communicating directly with Raven, but sadly it will always be a one-sided conversation. I talk about my day, things I wish to verbally share with Raven face to face. Sometimes I recap memories from the past when she was still here, as if to be reminiscing old times with her. What I would give to be able to sit and talk with her, there's so much I'd love to say, so many things we could laugh about together like we used to. I miss that so much.

The pennies we find remind us we carry Raven in our hearts

Raven was such a beautiful person, inside and out. She was a good baby, and the sweetest toddler ever. Her 1st day of school was a shocker. She'd been to daycare for a few years prior, so we expected her to fall right into the school environment. Padrick and I both had taken off work to be there for that first day. We stayed for a short time, and we couldn't help but to notice that Raven was being extremely clingy. When we tried to leave, she started crying which set a steady stream of tears flowing for me when we finally broke loose from the grip, she had on us both. Amazingly, Raven had the same kindergarten teacher that I had, Mrs. Helen Dobson. I'd requested her because I loved her when I had her, so I just knew that Raven would too. Mrs. Dobson picked Raven up that day and did her best to calm her as we left the room. I have a picture of that moment, and I'll treasure it forever.

Elementary school was awesome aside from the fact that Raven hated reading, and her dislike for reading became a nightly chore for me, as I'd also shared in a previous chapter. Reading was never really my thing either as I'd mentioned, but I'd suddenly found myself taking turns reading with Raven on school nights and sometimes weekends too. I'd ask her questions at the end of every chapter, even give her little test when the book was done. She did actually find a few series of books she enjoyed, Little Critter, Little Bear, Franklin and her favorite Ramona Quimby. We got to know each character well, she practically grew up with them as I see it.

School introduced Raven to much more than homework and endless reading assignments. It's where t-ball, coach pitch, softball, basketball and volleyball came into our lives. Raven loved playing sports. Her first taste of soccer wasn't the best, but with time it became her passion. Before we knew it, Raven was in high school where she later discovered a love for tennis too. Sometimes she'd leave one sport practice just to head off to another, but she enjoyed it, and we supported her in all that she did. She seemed to put a little more time and effort into soccer. I can remember her many times grabbing her soccer ball and heading over to the junior high playing field behind our house or running up and down the road we live on to stay in shape, she was that much into soccer. She really just had a natural talent for any sport she played.

High School academics was another story. It was rare to see Raven doing any homework or hear her even mention anything about upcoming assignments or tests. She did however struggle in Math, and we were certain of that. With lots of tutoring and one merciful teacher, she survived. I'm sad to say that she got those skills from me. Padrick is like a walking calculator. We could just throw out random numbers to him, and he's back with an answer in seconds, amazing! I like to call him the "tip master." That his specialty. I aspire to one day carry that skill, so far it isn't happening.

I guess we all can't be good at everything, but all of us have something we're good at. Raven was really good at writing, drawing too! She could write a good story. In her 10th grade English class, she had to keep a journal. The teacher would provide the topic, and the students would go from there. One entry required her to write about her most influential teacher, and she wrote about her math teacher Mrs. Stallings, and how much she helped and encouraged her in her math struggles. I made a copy of it, and I gave it to Mrs. Stallings sometime after Raven's accident. Reading it brought tears to her eyes, mine too! In another entry topic she was to write of her most favorite food. She wrote about the Del Rio, one of her favorite Mexican restaurants, and how much she loved the cheese dip and eating there on Sundays after church. We ate there the Sunday before Raven's accident; clueless it would be our last meal there together as a family. Not long after Raven's accident, I made a copy of what she had written about her love for the Del Rio. I added a picture of her, and I framed it. I gave it to the owners, and they gladly displayed it in a glass cabinet they had next to the cash register. I'm sad to report that 2019 brought an unexpected closing of the Del Rio. Padrick and I ate there often after Raven's accident. We were sure to go every year on her Anniversary date and Birthday. For her 9th Anniversary we hosted a Mexican Feast at our church in her memory. We got chips and salsa from the Del Rio as a part of the meal, and they were delicious! I have to think she was smiling down on us from Heaven. We do something big for her every year, so I can't help but to wonder if that one was her favorite so far.

Growing up as an only child, Raven often mentioned the desire to have a sibling, a little brother. Obviously, Padrick and I didn't fulfill that request. She always seemed to entertain herself well, although she enjoyed the fellowship of family and friends. Several years ago, Padrick and I sought out to sponsor a young boy through World Vision in memory of Raven. We were specific to search for one who shared the same birth date as her, August 10th. One was successfully located in Bolivia, South America. His name is Jesus. Since we began our sponsorship, we have enjoyed sending and receiving pictures and letters from Jesus, Raven's new little brother. He understands that he has a big sister in Heaven, and she's always watching over him.

Although Raven never got to attend her first prom, High School graduation, or move on into her college years, we did all that we could to make her a part of all that should have been, carrying her in our hearts every step of the way. Padrick and I attended both her proms and high school graduation. Her cousin and classmate Shannon was instrumental in helping us to make Raven a part of each. I never went to college myself, but for Raven, I spent 7 years as a part time student at a local Community College, getting 2 Associate Degrees in Raven's memory. Padrick who already holds degrees of his own, invested 3 years working to build what we call "The Bookie Barn" for Raven. It's a tiny home that holds a big piece of Raven in it. She'd always wanted a house with stairs, so now there's one built in her memory, and any who stay overnight take a little of Raven in their hearts when they leave. She is so loved, and in so many ways, remembered well.

Anniversary Memorial Setting at Church

I think the one thing I miss most about Raven is the sound of her laugher. She could get so tickled over the silliest things. Just hearing her laugh made me laugh, even if I were clueless as to exactly what happened to be so funny at the time. Sometime after Raven's accident, a friend and soccer mate of hers shared with Padrick and I a recording she had on her cell phone of Raven laughing. Just hearing it again was music to our ears. I can't even describe into words how it felt to hear her laughter again, especially after what seemed like so long. We saved the video and audio of that recording, and to this day we still go back and listen to it over and over again.

I don't think it would be fair to Raven to close out this book without lastly sharing of her love for animals. Raven loved all kinds of animals, but she was mostly the mother to cats. Her first love was a gray cat given to us by a neighbor. She named him Chance, and he was her very first best friend. I can remember so many times when she was little how she'd dress him in baby doll clothes, paint up his face with some play makeup, strap him into her doll stroller and push him around the house while wearing her plastic high heel shoes. It was the best ever. Sometimes she'd play hide and seek with Chance. She'd hide him in the dryer or shove him into our wooden drink holder in the kitchen, pretending "someone had left a kitty in her mailbox." That was her favorite line. He never fought her, he seemed to enjoy the attention. No matter what she did, he just loved her so much he would just sit there and let her do whatever made her happy. When she was happy, he was happy.

Raven had a few other cats Simba, Nala and Blue. They came into her life in that order. One Christmas Chance went missing. Being he was an indoor/outdoor cat, we sadly assumed he'd gotten run over somewhere by our house. We searched the neighborhood and never found him, then we were left to think someone had taken him. Raven was devastated, and we never found out what really happened to him, so soon after my mama found her another cat. It was a boy and he was orange, Raven's favorite color. We named him Simba, and he quickly became Raven's new best friend. She still missed Chance, but Simba just seemed to fill that gap losing Chance had left in her precious childhood. I loved seeing them play together, she just picked right up where her and Chance left off with Simba. He now was her new fur baby. He found himself being strapped in her doll stroller and pushed up and down the hallway. She started dressing him up and painting his face with her play makeup. It was great seeing her happy again. She fell in love with Simba, and he fell in love with her. Nala and Blue were her girl cats. Like Chance we lost Nala too. We have some good memories of her, but never found out what happened, and Raven was sad over that too. Blue was the last of Raven's cat crew. She'd gone missing the weekend before Raven's accident, and I can remember searching the neighborhood with her looking endlessly for her beloved cat Blue. Raven thought that maybe a neighbor had shot and killed Blue, but she showed up on our back porch the day after our search. I'm sad to report that we lost Blue the week after Raven's accident. Padrick found her on the road, but he didn't tell me until sometime later, knowing that I'd be upset, and I was. We still had Simba, and I can honestly say that he missed Raven so much! I can remember coming home from the hospital the evening of her accident. He stood at the doorway, waiting for Raven to come in with us, but she never did, it's like he knew something was wrong. For days, weeks and months after, just the mention of her name around him set him off. He'd sit up and look around for her, waiting, wondering where she was. It was the saddest thing to see, proof that animals grieve. In June of 2010 Simba was missing. Just like those before, Padrick and I searched out the neighborhood, asking if anyone had seen him, but nothing! I will go to my grave knowing in my heart that he was taken. I believe that of Chance too. I can't prove as to who, but I know that neither of those cats left on their own. They loved Raven too much to just leave. I have to think that if they've passed by this day and time that they're in Heaven with Raven, and if so, I know that are as happy as ever to be reunited with their mommy. I'm sure she has a mansion full of animals, cats and dogs of every kind and color. I can imagine that Sidney, Max, Molly and Lacey are in the mix, they were the dogs in her life. I can't wait to see for myself, and I know that I will one day. For now, I'll keep sharing stories of Raven with Layla and Miley, our 2 earthly fur babies who never met Raven, but hear her name often.

Although I have so many more stories and memories of Raven to have shared, I think I've covered a great deal in what I've chosen to write about in this book. My photo albums and journals will always hold the bulk of it all. I guess it's possible that you'd find some interest, or at the least be entertained by each, but my main goal in writing this book is to help someone in need, to let them know that surviving in loss is doable, even though it's not an easy task by any means. In closing, I'd like to say thank you. Thank you for your interest in my story, one I share with my husband Padrick. Thank you for your commitment to read this book from start to finish, however short or long it may have been for you personally. My goal was to cover what I felt to be important details without losing you as the reader. Our experience of loss has been and continues to be a daily struggle. If you share in this loss or in the event that you do, I pray that this book will contribute in some way to your healing process. Everyone grieves differently.

There's no set time or list of expectations to check off, although I strongly advise keeping a journal to record your progress. I have journaled of this journey for some time now, and my intention is to continue. Sometimes I look back through old entries just to see where I was compared to where I am now. I will say that the passing of time does tend to soften the blow a little, but life as it once was will never be the same again. Keeping your mind and body busy can be hugely instrumental in surviving in the loss of a child, that and the support of family and friends. Of course, the most important advice I can give is to keep yourself as close to God as possible. Pray, pray and pray some more. Stay closely connected to your church family, and if you don't have one, get one! I can't imagine doing this on my own, or not allowing the Lord and His people to help carry me every step of the way. Padrick and I have no choice but to trust God completely in this. We cling to the hope we have through Jesus, and we focus on the promise that we will see Raven again one day in Heaven. Every passing day brings us one day closer to a sweet, sweet reunion, and that gives us both something to look forward to as we live out our days in this life till the Lord returns or calls us home. I'll say it once again, Hallelujah! Praise the Lord and thank you Jesus! Our weeping may last for a night, but Joy is coming in the morning!

Raven and her cat Simba

Jesus gives us the "Hope"
that we will see Raven again
for All Eternity John 3:16

Printed in the United States
by Baker & Taylor Publisher Services